Coffee with Colby

365 Days Of Fresh Brewed Spirit Inspiration!

COLBY REBEL

The information in this book is intended as a guide for starting and building your own spiritual practice. Neither the author, Publishing or anyone associated with Psychic Senses claim it is a substitute for professional or medical services.

Cover Design: Georgi Petrov

Cover Illustration: Lizzie Martell

ISBN-13: 978-0-578-68087-3
ISBN-10: 0-578-68087-4

COFFEE WITH COLBY
365 Days Of Fresh Brewed Spirit Messages

COLBY REBEL

This book is dedicated to my grandmother, Jane Clauser, who continues to guide, inspire and encourage me every day. She motivates me to be the absolute best version of myself in every way possible and has been truly supportive of my path with Spirit. To be a witness to her strength, character and resiliency is inspiring beyond words. I feel so blessed to be a recipient of her love. It is an absolute privilege to have such a powerful and inspirational woman in my life to show me what's truly important in this physical experience. We even share the love of a nice French roast.

Message From Spirit

You are the pulse. The pulse of the physical world that is desperately needed to manifest all of the potential we see.

You are the good and the light. We see that in you. When you center and when you remember is when you see that within you as well. You have the power to raise others. We ask that you use this power to motivate and inspire those around you.

Your tools are your smile, warmth, kindness, gentleness, strength, resilience and passion. Your gift is the ability to get up even after feeling broken. Allow your soul to glow so those who are lost will come to you for safety. Be that light for others.

It is through your compassion and kindness you can create a chain reaction of healing and hope and show that we can all come together.

We understand that this may be a of year reflection to review and check in, but it is also a year of guidance. Moving forward with our messages of guidance.

As you reflect on years past and as you move forward, we ask that you do not forget to check in on your entire soul's journey. Look at all of the glorious places your soul has visited. Remembrance of all those you've helped through each soul experience.

You are glorious. You are a healer. You are loved. May you take your light out to love as many as you can. Show those who feel desolate that there is a hope for them. Carry them with your love. Your heart is big enough. Do not worry. Show them there is a way, and that way is through love.

Express your emotions, do not allow fear to hold you back. Open your heart without apology. For those that have hurt you will have their own accord so do not give them the gift of dimming your light.

Carry your head high and remember your purpose. You are here to light the path and to create a space of love that does not have limits. You are limitless in your ability to love and boundless in to how you choose to share that love.

You are the chariot. Know we are with you as we are your family, we are your friends, we are your soul and we are your spirit. Carry us close and feel the love we give to you this day and every day.

Preface

Do you ever feel those nudges from the Universe? The ones that make you begin to question your path? Do you ever wish you could hear guidance a little bit more clearly? This is the beginning of understanding that there is more to this physical world. There is a spiritual realm that exists among us. It's all around us like air, but yet, we don't always see it. There are times when your senses may tune in and just know that there is an energy around you, or perhaps, you feel it, see it or hear it. These are your senses picking up on that energy, that spirit realm.

This realm is both loving and supportive. They are our family, friends, teachers and pets. They may be our angels or guides. They wish to help us along our path. They now see the uselessness in fear and self-sabotage and work diligently to show us true love, passion and light.

Coffee with Colby is filled with those messages from those guides and angels. The messages that inspire, motivate and encourage you to live your purpose and release the fear you carry within.

Insightful and sound advice is how some may describe the messages as Spirit does its part to make them practical and informative for anyone who may need a personal message at any given point in their day.

It's now time to tune into that guidance and listen to your own intuition with each and every message. To start your day in the highest vibration possible so that you may begin to manifest those dreams that you've been suppressing and to start to see yourself in a new light. A light of self-love and greatness and magnificence that Spirit sees you in. A light that has no limits, no boundaries and no time for procrastination. Now is YOUR time to begin living your purpose with *Coffee with Colby* there to guide and inspire you.

Acknowledgements

There are so many to thank for this spiritual journey. I have been blessed to have been supported by Spirit and the Universe as I make my way through this physical experience as a soul being. Many lessons have been learned, but my unbreakable trust and commitment to Spirit has led me to this book today. Although there are so many to thank, here's just a few that I'd like to express my most sincere gratitude and appreciation for those that have truly inspired and helped to manifest this book!

The Rebel Pack,

First and foremost, I want to give thanks to *YOU*, the Rebel Pack. You are the followers, the supporters and the fans that have committed yourself to watching the weekly *Coffee with Colby* videos and supporting me every step of the way for these last several years. You literally inspired this book, and I am and will be forever grateful for your loyalty, love and support! Thank you for your follows, views and positive messages you give each and every day!

Mavis Pittilla,

Thank you for demonstrating the power of spirit with your inspirational talks and messages. You have been such an inspiration on channeling the divine and have set a standard of serving spirit with the highest regard.

Lizzie Martell,

It's incredible how a chance meeting can create a beautiful bond. Spirit brought you into my life as they knew you would be the one to help me express their visions the best. Thank you for all of your hard work with the three book covers. Thank you for always creating the time and space needed to make these visions a reality. You are such a blessing.

Robin De Lano and Nicole Dionne,

What can I say? This book could not have been done without your beautiful gifts and commitment. Thank you for your endless hours of watching the videos and for your relentless commitment to compiling the words in exact form and with such grace and power.

With Gratitude,

Colby

Introduction

What if you had a chance to receive a divine message from the Universe and your guides every day? Well, now you can with *Coffee with Colby*! Coffee with Colby has been a live podcast for over three years. Every week, Colby channels a message from Spirit and delivers it live. This book is a collection of inspirational messages channeled from Spirit meant to guide, motivate and inspire you on your journey!

This is a book to help you connect to your guides, higher-self and the Universe on a daily basis. It serves as a reminder that you have a purpose and to release any fear or insecurities you may have towards moving towards that purpose with confidence and passion.

There are many books that offer 365 pages of quotes, but none offer the practical push that *Coffee with Colby* does in its approach to stretch you outside of your comfort zone.

These messages are not your ordinary airy fairy fluff, but rather practical talk from Spirit and your guides offering you comforting and uplifting messages. Some will give you the push you need. The messages are positive and supportive. Regardless of what you may be experiencing at this moment in your life, these messages will help you with healing and clarity.

Every message has been channeled and delivered to you in a way that will feel personal. In fact, you may feel as if your guides are talking directly to you. Trust that each message you receive is exactly the message you need at this time. Now it's time to begin your journey with Spirit!

How To Use This Book

Begin your day by grabbing your cup of joe and communicating with your guides and the Universe using this book as your tool!

This book can be used in a multitude of ways.

Option 1: Simply sit and read each message from Day #1 to Day #365. Trust that each message that day is the message intended for you to help you on your path and journey!

Option 2: Feeling stuck or just need a bit of inspiration? You may use the book as a divination tool by asking a question to your guides and the Universe, then open the book randomly to any page to see what message they have for you!

Option 3: Read the book front to back taking in *ALL* of the messages at once. Fill your soul with the love, support and nurturing it needs to give you a solid foundation and kick start to your year. Then, choose a daily message for each day.

Every page offers an uplifting message and it may just be a nudge from your guides to get going on your path!

From faith in the spirit world, connecting to your intuition, releasing fear, purging and relationships. Every page offers an inspirational and motivational message that sets a positive and healing tone as you begin your day.

This book also functions as an oracle tool, as you can ask a question to your guides or universe and open the book to a specific message that provides guidance, support, answers, and encouragement.

Coffee with Colby will be the support you need on a daily basis and on an as-needed basis to lend you the guidance and direction to help you release blocks, remove fear and be inspired to take those next steps on your path!

Start Your Day with
a Big Big Cup of Coffee

Day #1

Congratulations on entering a new year in your physical world. We hope you see all that is coming for you. We want you to allow your light to shine **brighter** than you ever have before.

To **embrace** this new year as a **new** beginning. We have given you another 365 opportunities.

What will you choose to do with them?

Day #2

When you come into the living, you are *given* choices. However, if you choose to stay still, to not move, then you can't expect something *new* to happen.

Day #3

Ask yourself:

What's the one thing I can clear out of my spiritual junk drawer today?

What belief system am I holding on to that no longer serves my highest good?

What am I telling myself, that in all honesty, is not truth but ego playing games with me?

Day #4

When you feel the urge to try something new that is us giving you the *inspiration*. The *nudge* needed to move you forward. Your greatness is already there, it is the *light within* waiting to be nurtured.

Day #5

If you have been broken by another, we have only done that to show you how resilient your *love* can be. So that you can see you are stronger than the pain you feel. The pain will be temporary, but love is forever. This is why we have also shown *unconditional* love. We wish for you to see this within self-love as well. To love yourself fully and unconditionally.

Day #6

Remember, each time you have experienced a failure, set-back, heartache or disappointment, those experiences are meant to move you *forward*. They are *not* meant to push you back.

Day #7

You are meant to *experience emotions*. You are meant to go through the process of grief and heartache to show you how resilient you are and that through it all, you are truly meant to *love*.

Day #8

Chasing people and situations is *wasted* energy.

Go inwards and focus on *WHO* and *WHAT* is important.

When giving your energy, make sure it's *appreciated* and *reciprocated*.

Day #9

Vague is *vengeful*. When you honor and uphold this belief to being *clear* in your communication with others, you will live a more *authentic, honest* and *heart-centered* life.

Day #10

You worry if you'll succeed or if those around you will be satisfied. We want to remind you that you are already *successful*. You have endured this incredible journey into a physical body and a physical world and are learning to how to use the *GPS* to *navigate*.

Day #11

Expand your energetic reach to hug as many as you possibly can within your *physical* and *spiritual* experience.

You will see that in the end it was not about any sadness, loss or disappointment.

It is about how great you are willing to *love* regardless of all of those other emotions that attempted to derail your *true* purpose.

Day #12

*The **power** to **empower**.* How are you talking to yourself? How are you honoring, celebrating, and supporting yourself?

Do you spend your time negating yourself, giving yourself a hard time? This does nothing but lower your own confidence.

Why would you do that?

If you can't be in your own corner, how can you expect anyone else to be in your corner?

Day #13

If something *feels* like a struggle, it may be that *spirit* is giving you that experience so you can help others.

Take that experience, turn it into a positive and *pay it forward*.

Day #14

When you are open to **allowing** your story to change, the **universe** has more access, tools, and opportunity to them, to bring your **dreams** to you.

Day #15

You have this beautiful *opportunity* to connect *to* your higher self and your soul. If you truly listen and date your soul, you will *NEVER* again feel off track.

Why would you *not* want to do that?

Day #16

You are so *powerful*.

And when you *know* that and *believe* that from your soul, there are *no limits*.

Day #17

Each day ask yourself the following questions:

What is the opportunity presented to me today?

Where can I find that opportunity?

How can I manifest that opportunity?

How can I pull that into my energy, my aura, my existence?

Day #18

Emotional Arthritis:

Ask yourself…

Do I have it?

Where is it?

How am I holding on to it?

How am I feeding it?

Is my belief system feeding it?

How can I release it?

Day #19

Are your expectations reasonable?

If your expectations aren't reasonable, you'll consistently feel disappointed. You'll feel as if you're not enough simply because your expectations are too high, or the expectations of others are too high.

Day #20

Take any possible opportunity to *give back*. When you give, you alleviate stress and fill your *heart with love*.

In the moment of giving, you're simultaneously forgetting about your struggle.

It's a nice way to *escape* for a bit, while giving back in a *positive* way.

Day #21

You may concern yourself that won't have the energy to hold the space for so many, but we remind you that you are an *infinite* being that has no limitations. Any limits you perceive are within your mind, but ***not*** within your ***soul***.

Day #22

Think about this –
If you could only write down
and record what you say about
yourself, and that is all anyone
would hear about you;

What would they hear?
What would they think about you?

It's quite a reality check when
you look at it that way.

Day #23

We see times when you are feeling *alone* and *lonely*. When you experience a sadness that is deep within and *unexplainable*. We see your sense of loss. We *encourage* you to go deep within your soul to *remember* the experience prior to the physical realm and allow those imprints of love and *connection* you once felt, to embrace you. Your soul remembers the *unconditional* love and support from us.

Day #24

So rather than creating an excuse and wasting time, *allow* this time for yourself to *grow* and *evolve*. Allow yourself to be creative and think outside the box. Take those *moments* for things that you hadn't created space for previously.

Day #25

MANTRA for today:

*I refuse to get in my own way.
I refuse to procrastinate.
I CHOOSE to take positive action.*

Find the joy in *celebrating* your soul assignments, celebrating your next steps.

Day #26

You are enough. You're more than enough. You're *infinite*.

Think about that. You are **INFINITE**! It is THAT easy when you own it.

Day #27

Your **soul** is **beautiful** and when you feel disconnected, we will gently guide you back to your *all-knowing self*. **Trust** us during these difficult time as we have never left you. Even in your doubt, we are always here giving you that **nudge** when needed.

Day #28

When you are in alignment with your soul, it's easy. *Choices* are easy. *Decisions* are easy. *Love* is easy. When you are within your soul, you won't feel a sense of failure.

When something feels off or even if you are just having a bad day, get back into *alignment* with your soul. In that moment, you will absolutely see how quickly your day will turn around.

Day #29

When you are in **balance** you have **endless** energy. You feel amazing. When you **begin** to feel deprived, lethargic and depressed around simple **circumstances**, it's a sign you are out of balance and need to realign.

Day #30

You have to **LOVE** yourself first, take care of yourself first, *honor* who you are, *honor* what you want, *honor* your *boundaries* and be able to *stand* in your power when doing so. You will find that when you do that, you start *manifesting* and calling in *those things you want.*

Day #31

When you stand up for yourself, you create **different** energy. You will *bring* in people that respect you and *lose* those that don't. *That's okay right? Do you need those people in your circle?* **No.** You don't. **STAND UP** for what you want. SPEAK UP. *Use your voice.*

Day #32

Each day ask yourself these questions?

Have I shown spirit my gratitude today? What can I do today to serve spirit?

Start by sitting with spirit with a sense of presence and gratitude.

GRATITUDE for how much the spirit world is taking care of you and remembering your loved ones in spirit are watching over you.

WHAT ARE YOU
Grateful for?

Day #33

If you *focus* your energy forward it moves *forward*. Think of someone and *IMAGINE* yourself standing directly in front of them while sending them love. Say to yourself *My heart to your heart*.

They are going to *RECEIVE* that love and they will actually *feel* it. It's the same thing with spirit. Send your energy out to spirit, they are going to *feel* that energy.

Day #34

When you say *goodbye* to old relationships, it's an opportunity to say *hello* to new ones and to see why spirit is bringing them to you.

Those *new* relationships stepping in are for the *next level* or the *next chapter* of your life because your vibration has shifted.

Day #35

Let yourself *grow*. Let yourself *expand*. Know who you are. When you know who you are, you always know what to do.

It's about going inward and saying to yourself:

I know who I am.

I know what I am about.

I am going to trust and honor that.

Spirit will have your back!

Day #36

It's hard losing a relationship. You have to **grieve** it. It can feel like a death to you. Especially if that person was there *helping* you along the way, *lifting* you up and particularly when you weren't expecting it. When you *fully understand* that this is about spirit showing you that your **soul contract** with that relationship has ended it can help you move on.

Day #37

We ask that you allow your soul to be *free* from all of the self-doubts you have placed on it. Let your *love* wash away your fears.

Feel the sun melt your doubts.

You are caging the greatest gift we gave you, your *soul*.

You are a *miracle* manifested to provide *hope* and *light* to others.

Day #38

Use your voice for **celebration** and **empowerment**, rather than detrimental negative self-talk or gossip. **Speak** empowering words, think empowering thoughts and feel loving actions. When you **encompass** this as a practice, you are naturally going to **rise**. You will keep **lifting** yourself and those around you.

Day #39

In order to manifest what you want you must **move** towards it. You *can't* expect things to just *fall into your lap*. The work you do and putting forward is allowing the Universe to help you **manifest** and bring in the opportunities that you are seeking.

Day #40

SPIRIT is throughout the world. There are many people **serving spirit** all around the world. It's a *reminder* that all of us are **connected** each and every day.

Day #41

No more secrets. Secrets *hurt* people no matter what. When you know something, ask yourself:

Am I holding a secret?
Should I share it?

If it's something to share have the courage to share it. Share it with *empathy* and *compassion*. Share it with **LOVE**. Just do your part. We've all got to do our part.

Day #42

We ask that today and every day you *honor your soul* with the **love** and care that we did when we gave it to you.

You do not need protection for we are here, and you can simply reach out to us in your *times of need*.

Day #43

You have your **spirit guides** all around you. But what *limitations* are you placing on yourself within that relationship? Are you *believing* in it or interfering with that connection? So, ask yourself what are you doing? Are you *supporting* or *disrupting* your connection?

Day #44

There are many times where you may feel **lost**. You may feel **afraid** or **abandoned**.

It's in these times for you to **dig deep** and **trust**.

Your guide may just be standing behind you or right beside you.

Day #45

You keep looking. You ask your guide *Where are you? Why can't I see you?* Maybe your guide is busy watching your back and taking care of you and doesn't have time to stand in front of you. This is about trust in knowing they are with you.

Day #46

Be *focused* and **detailed** about what you want and go beyond wishing on a vision board. Put thought into what you want and **CREATE** a plan. Understand the steps that are *needed* and *start* to implement those steps. Your dreams won't fall into your lap, you must *work* for them. What's so amazing about this, is it's *going to work*!

Day #47

Desire success? **Remove** excuses. That's the *first* thing. Own when you're making an excuse. Then ask yourself,

Why am I making this excuse? Where does this belief come from?

Those excuses may be an indicator that additional *inner work* is needed.

Day #48

In your acts of **KINDNESS** in giving to one another, you are *pure love*, exemplifying all that we desire, all that we created. We are always surrounding you with the **GREATEST** love you can possibly *imagine*.

Day #49

ASK yourself:

Who can you support? Who has some wings that need some lifting? How can you support them?

You have the *power* to lift those around you and each time you do, you lift yourself in the process.

Day #50

DON'T be afraid to spend time with yourself. Sometimes you may *avoid* that, right? You avoid it because the *truth* comes out. Once you know the truth, it's difficult because you know *change is coming*.

Rather than holding back and being fearful of the change, try *celebrating* the change and feel positive about it?

Day #51

Take the time to say:

Why am I uncomfortable?
What is bothering me?
And what can I do about it?

Rather than *focusing* on what you can't do, focus on what you can. What <u>can</u> you do?

Day #52

In order to move **FORWARD,** in order to *grow*, spirit has you *reflect* so you can *purge*. Spirit is pushing the old out of you. They are sitting there letting you process all of that. It's like the gunk at the bottom, right? Spirit has you purge so you can *release* it and *let it go*. This opens the door for the 2.0 version of you to come in.

Day #53

We want **YOU** to be there for one another because, you are supposed to. You are *not* supposed to go through this experience *alone*.

Day #54

Remember that you are **not** here to judge. You are not here to wave a finger. You are simply here to *work this life out* like everybody else. This gives you a moment of perspective to **relate** and **empathize** with what another person is going through and to be cautious of assumption of another.

Day #55

WHEN you get too busy on your daily routine, take a moment and **STOP** yourself. Feel that *presentness* and feel that ground under you. Then just take a beat and say, *Thank you* to someone you cross paths with. You will *never* know the **IMPACT** that it may have on someone else's life. Just a simple *thank you*.

Day #56

Think about your day-to-day operations and say to yourself;

I am going to show up. I'm going to be there. *I'm going to represent.* I am *choosing* to represent *myself* today.

Day #57

Solitude is really a *fabulous opportunity* to understand what it is you want, rather than being misguided because you are not tuning into your own soul. Your inward time is so *precious*. By *going inward*, you connect to your soul and your higher self. When *feeling lost*, spend time in solitude to *find* your way *home* again.

Day #58

WHEN you show up, *each and every* time and the more you do it, the more you say **yes** to the universe, the more you **keep** your **promises** and **keep** your **appointments**, the more you find that *self-discipline* the more you will **manifest** what you are putting out.

Day #59

If you **continue** to make **excuses** you will *fail to make progress*. If you find yourself making excuses time and time again, you have to be *strong enough* to be **accountable**.

Day #60

PEEL away the layers that are holding you back. Peel away fear, anxiety, failure, disappointment. *Don't worry* about what your friends and family are going to say. It's your *responsibility* to make the most of your *physical experience*.

Day #61

In that time off when you're not needing to punch a clock, take those moments and *take time for yourself* to look at what you want.

What is your *intuition* telling you? What is your *spirit calling* for? And *answer* it.

Day #62

Too often we are taking our own lives and our own happiness for granted. It's time to say, **no more** it's time to take a stand and say:

I matter. I count. And when I'm there for me, I can be there for others.

Day #63

Starting off each morning with a solid **15 minutes** of *focused meditation*, will **radically** change your happiness and your well-being.

Day #64

TODAY we *celebrate* you. You are a *beautiful* source of light with a soul that *emanates* all that is *good* in the world.

Day #65

You **MUST** put yourself *first*. I know that sounds hard. It may even sound selfish, but it isn't. *When* you put yourself first, you are *feeding* yourself first, *putting* your mask on you first, and you will *always* make sure your tank is *full*. When your tank is full you have so much more to *offer* others.

Day #66

Are you *cherishing* your life now? The more you wait, the more you are *wasting* what **SPIRIT** is *giving* you.

Day #67

You have to **open** those **fear** boxes. Open up the chambers where you lock things away so you can **create** space to let something **new** come into your vibration. Allow something new to step into your **awareness**.

Day #68

IF you trust them, you trust what they are ***giving***, what you are given, and *you trust* the ***connection*** is there.

Trust that your loved ones are around. When you *hear* a song or *see* a symbol, ***trust*** that it's from your ***loved one***. Why keep testing them?

Day #69

WHEN you become **comfortable** with being **uncomfortable**, that is your *SWEET* spot for GROWTH.

Day #70

When you feel really **passionate** about something, you will have more energy, dedication and focus around it. You will have a **desire** to continuously work on it and you won't get bored. You will **manifest** more because of all that hard work you are doing. Start with **passion** and let the rest *fall into place.*

Day #71

What would *you* be willing to truly dedicate yourself to? When you *discover* what that is and dedicate yourself fully, the doors will start to open for you. *Opportunities* will be presented. You got to do your part with it, as always, but your *dedication* will take you far.

Day #72

Even in your **darkest** moments we ask that you not sit with doubt, but to **stand with love**. To **realize** that we are with you and can be called upon in any moment you need. Rather than walk your physical experience alone, ask others to walk with you. **Gather** those around you and let them know you are in great need of support. **Reach out** to help those who may need an **extra** lift today.

Day #73

Your **perceived** failure or set back is a LESSON to push you **forward**, not hold you back.

Day #74

THERE are those that will walk with a dark heart. This is not *personal* to you. This is their pain. When you see this pain, *embrace* them with love. Your soul is your *gift* and *spirit* is your source in which to use this gift to *transform* the darkness to light.

The pain to *love*.

Day #75

LET your *inner* self out *more*. *Believe* in your own *self-worth*. Stop feeling like others are more worthy than you. Tune into your *higher self*. Ground and center. BE willing to look inward. If there are things you want to work on and grow, spend time doing that. Spend time *building* your own worth. *You are your own Empire.*

Day #76

This collective **collaboration** that we consider life and spirit is designed like the squares to a quilt. Each square **must** be different to bring dimension and **uniqueness** to the quilt. Each square is needed to complete that quilt. **No** two squares are the same. Nor will **any** quilt ever be **complete**, if all of the squares don't participate in the **experience**.

Day #77

BECAUSE of all your experiences you are **stronger**, you are **smarter**, you are more **intuitive** than you were the year before. With **each** experience you have, you **grow** your **intuitive** senses. **Celebrate** those **experiences**. The *GOOD* and the *BAD*.

Day #78

If you are **dedicated** and follow through, you will see *transition*. It's *not* overnight. Most times it's a lot of work, time, effort, **patience** and tears. *Sometimes it's screaming into a pillow.* Other times it's asking, **What am I doing?**

But then, there are those magic times of knowing, 'I am **exactly** where I am **supposed** to be.'

Day #79

Maybe it's all about making sure you still *move* forward, *even* if you're **forced** to sit still during the **process**.

Day #80

When you put *pressure* on yourself, you're not going to get the *answers* that you're seeking. Answers come in the *quiet* moments. Answers come when you are willing to be *still* and ground. When you choose to *surrender* and *release* any preconceived notions of what it's *supposed* to be about.

Day #81

LET yourself *develop* through what you *love*. Let yourself develop through what is *natural* for you.

Day #82

When a relationship is over, be **clear** with that person. It shows **integrity** and **honesty**. You are letting them know exactly how you feel and what's on your mind. It's important to **uphold** this because if you don't then you will only **mislead** and leave a sense of *holding onto someone* or worse yet, making them *hold on to you*.

Day #83

If there's a place you want to go, a place you've been thinking about or have always wanted to explore, see how you can make that happen for yourself. *Do it* in a way that tells the Universe

I'm not going to quit.
I'm going to live.
I am doing this.

Allow your soul to explore.

Day #84

YOUR success isn't dependent on other people; your success is dependent on *your belief in yourself*. Are you putting yourself out there? Are you showing up when you're being called to action? Are you taking those *leaps of faith*?

Day #85

YOU have to *own* where you are and own what's **realistic** in your approach. *Own* your *boundaries* and your expectations. **Push** yourself and push hard, but *not* to the point where your **expectations** are **unreasonable**. Make sure you are *managing* your energy with **self-love**.

Day #86

Understanding Anxiety vs. Intuition

Anxiety:

Percolates or seeps into causing worry or negativity.

Intuition:

Pops into awareness a random thought, feeling or image that's almost inspirational.

Day #87

WHEN you are **connected** to your **higher self** and allow that higher self to **nurture** the **physical self**, you will feel **less** alone.

Day #88

WHEN you are *pulled* out of your element you **struggle** with **surrendering** because you are trying to hold on to what you know. You are trying to hold on to what brings you **comfort**. During these times, it's the art of surrendering and **releasing** that **creates** space and allows the **flow** to happen.

Day #89

Your guides may be trying to *redirect* you into something new. This may be a new path or *revelation*. They may be helping you to *purge* or aiding you in *healing*. It's through that pushing and through that guiding you begin to see the bigger picture. It's through that, you can start to see where you are being *guided*.

Day #90

Being FORCED to stay in is a wonderful *opportunity* to practice surrendering, to allow yourself to look at your life and reflect. It's the *perfect* opportunity to ask yourself

Am I where I am supposed to be?

Rather than being eager to get back to your routine, ask yourself if that routine worked for you? Is that routine *fulfilling* within your soul?

Day #91

Don't **live** your life in victim mode. Living your life in victim mode **prevents** you from *growing* and *healing*. You'll continuously **perpetuate** the story that you tell yourself.

Find your inner **survivor** and live **that** life.

Day #92

WE have *given* you so many *miracles* to see that *reflection* of goodness in all that is upon you. In the darkest hours, you have within you the *power* to not only *see* the good, but to be the *good*.

Day #93

You're *stronger* than you give yourself credit for. *Braver* than you believe. *Grittier* than you realize. When you get down to it and put your *faith* in you, you'll *discover* that you can truly *change* and *maximize* your course. It does take that listening. It does take that *surrendering*. But as you do it, you will start to free yourself and find your *destiny*.

Day #94

The **key** is this, if that story is not working for you, get rid of it. **Purge it**. If you are holding onto something physically and you **no longer** need it, **get rid** of it. Purge it. If you are holding to a relationship that is no longer serving you, get rid of it. **Purge** that too.

Day #95

We will TEST you along this path you are taking. Some tests may be quick quizzes while others feel like a final exam. This is done to **prevent** you from becoming *comfortable, complacent* and *content*. We want you to **shift** and **grow** and to **learn** to find happiness and joy throughout **each** stage of your life.

Day #96

When you *discover* your own
magic and see it within you, you
can then share it with others.
That is truly *inspiring*. That is
what will create the *change*
within and help you to realize
you're making a *difference*.

Day #97

You can be **grateful** for your experiences, the good, and the bad. You **learn** and you **grow** through those challenges.

You dig **deep**, get gritty and find what you are made of. But you don't need to hang on to them. You don't have to keep **holding** on to that pain, sorrow or regret. You don't have to hold on to the guilt. Let it go.

Day #98

We will *give* you wings when you need them, we will also give you the *push* when you are behind on your life plan. We will *celebrate* with you in victory and we will cry with you during a *perceived* defeat. But remember, there is *no* defeat nor no failure. There is only where we have taken you to be your *truest* self.

Day #99

Figure out how you can share that love, *share* that light, share that positivity. Because *believe* it or not there might be something that you say that you share, that *helps* get someone through a difficult situation or a difficult circumstance.

Day #100

WHEN you *see* someone around you who seems to be in need, *offer* help to them. It may be a kind word, a bit of food or a listening ear. When you *remember* that you are *abundant* you can give *without* fear of lack.

Day #101

Going *beyond* what you think.
Going beyond what you *feel*.
Going beyond distracting
yourself or *occupying* yourself.
Go deep deep deep *into* your
soul and to see if there is any
healing that still needs to be
done.

Day #102

Do you think the universe is trying to hold you back? Do you think the universe is saying, *Oh, no not you sweetie? We're going give it to <u>her</u> over there, but <u>not</u> you.*

They are *not* doing that. You are doing that to yourself.

Day #103

When you go about it with a sense of saying, *I'm going to trust, I'm going to surrender, I'm going to embrace.*

Then *no matter what* is given to you it's actually not so overwhelming. It's when you are resisting that it becomes so overwhelming.

Day #104

LOOK at hurdles as a *positive* thing! The more you jump them, the more you get over and the more you accomplish. The more you accomplish the more *confidence* you build. You will then see that the whole world doesn't crumble around you, *even* if, it felt like it in that moment. YOU can *overcome*. YOU can *surpass* your own fear.

Day #105

WHEN you *find* yourself, all wrapped up in worry and getting into your head. *Stop yourself*. Have enough self-control and self-discipline to pull yourself out of that self-sabotaging mindset. *Focus* on *embracing* the change with positive light and positive love. It will make all the *difference*. You will see.

DON'T WORRY BE HAPPY

Day #106

YOU may *prefer* purging your closet than purging your soul. But it's got to be done. *You know why?* Because, it's what takes you to the *next* level. It's how you are going to become a *new* person. A person *feeling* stronger, better, refreshed. Feeling like you've *accomplished* something, *because you have.*

Day #107

Narcissists *love* to play mind games. They think they are smarter than you. They'll **manipulate** any situation in order to make their viewpoint the *right one*. Many times, a narcissist will try their best to make you feel guilty. It's important to **stand** your ground and **own** your truth in these confrontational encounters.

Day #108

This is an **opportunity**, for you to share your **love**, to share your **light** and to **share** your kindness to bring people **together**. To **remember** that although you may *never* know what someone is going through, you have **enough** love within to **help** make a difference.

Together

Day #109

We are **stronger** together. Life may be a simple test, for us all to experience as one. Look at what role you can play. In this moment try *sending out love*. **Raise** that vibration by **focusing** on joy, happiness, and gratitude. You will **help** so many of those struggling to find those things at this moment.

Day #110

GO *inwards*. Find your unique voice. *Explore* what makes you different. When you do that you will be *true* to you. Your *essence* will be in *alignment* with that. Then nobody can ever duplicate you. *Nobody*.

Day #111

It is through the **darkness** that you **find** your light. In despair you find your **strength**, and, in your sorrow, you find **love**. Remember that you are loved. We are sending you love and **guiding** you along your journey. You are not alone on your path of **love** and **enlightenment**.

Day #112

STOP telling yourself those *stories* that *reinforce* belief systems that are *not* serving your *highest* good.

Day #113

Empathize with the imitator, *the one who takes from another,* because they are *not* experiencing *freedom*. They are not *trusting*. They are not trusting themselves. They are *not* trusting their gift. They are not trusting their connection. They are not trusting *Spirit*; *therefore,* they resort to imitation.

Day #114

Shine your light. Don't be afraid to **share** it. Don't be afraid to **express** it.

Shine your light and shine it bright.

Day #115

Are you **holding** on to something from years ago? **Give** yourself that **love** and **opportunity** to work on it. To **heal** it, *once and for all* so you can **move on**.

Day #116

The MOST important thing is to stay *motivated*. That means getting up early, setting the alarm, getting out of bed, making the bed, getting out of your pajamas, putting clothes on, taking that shower, getting yourself ready. That's going to help KEEP you motivated. Start your day like any other day. Start your day with a *plan*.

Show up for yourself.

Day #117

You're **hunting** for the answers.
You're hunting for your **purpose**.
When you **dig deep** you will find
it and you will free yourself.
You're going to **lighten** yourself
up. It's not going to be fun, but
you've got **nothing** else to lose so
you might as well **get to it**.

Day #118

There are a lot of things that you can be doing. *Take* your days to research, learn, absorb, grow, and then grow some more. This sets you up for **success**. You will be in a place of *moving forward* and not in a place of **catching up**.

Day #119

Getting yourself together and getting yourself **connected** and finding ways to keep that connection **growing** strong is so important. Learn and **understand** how much you need a *spiritual community* beyond social media. **Find** those people and places that you resonate with and can participate in. Where it feels like **home** to your soul.

Day #120

Look at how many **different** things you've done in your life. Have you ever tried something, but you didn't stick with it? Don't **disqualify** those experiences. You will be *shocked and surprised* at how much those experiences come **back** into your life to help you when you're on track with your life purpose.

Day #121

There are those days you want to pull the blankets over your head, but you can't. You have to get up and say *Hey, it's my time*.

Exercise your self-discipline and you will to move forward. *Remove* any fears that you have created for yourself.

Say to yourself *I am capable of doing this. I am worthy of this. It's my time.*

Day #122

It really comes down to **owning** and **trusting** your all-knowing self, your **higher self** that *whispers* and *nudges* you. That **encourages** you to keep going.

Day #123

Stop and ask yourself if you are trying your best. Are you saying to the world, *This is who I am?* It starts with *you* telling the world who you are, what you represent, what you believe in. Standing up and saying:

'If you don't like it, then you're just not meant for me.'

Day #124

How do you **discover** your *life purpose*? How do you know if you are on track? *Don't overthink it.* **Look** at yourself and write down anything you would **enjoy** doing. You know they say do what you would do for **free**? In a way that does make sense. Ask **yourself** what comes natural to you?

That is your sign.

Day #125

Everyone has a block somewhere in their life. Whether it's your *finances, relationship, career, self-confidence,* anything. At some point you will have a **block** that **holds** you back. This is an opportunity for you to **pinpoint** where this block began and to **choose** whether or not to dislodge it from your thought patterns.

Day #126

YOU are *meant* to be in your *light* and *stand* in your *power*. To help others and to *own* who you are in the most *positive* way.

Day #127

FREE yourself from these *obligations* that don't even fulfill you. Why are you *plugging* along for something that doesn't even bring you joy? One of the most *beautiful* things that can come out of your *experience,* is figuring out what really is important to you. *What* is that for you?

Day #128

This is a **golden** opportunity for **inner** work. That inner work is what's going to **create** peace and create balance for you. **When** you have that **balance**, you are going to be able to go through those *ups* and *downs* **without** feeling deprived. Without **feeling** like something is missing.

Day #129

At the end of the day,
it has got to come from within.
A mindset of

I'm going to show up
and be there today.

It doesn't matter whether or not you *feel* like it. It's about being *accountable*. *Each* time you are accountable and *every* time you show up, whether it's for yourself, someone else, or spirit, you are telling the universe,

I am ready. I deserve this.

Day #130

Take that time to say

What can I work on within?
What am I struggling with?
And how do I move past it?

Day #131

Stop **navigating** your world around making sure other people are happy. Making sure you don't *ruffle* feathers and staying **inside** the lines. **Let go** of playing it safe and push yourself to the brink, push yourself to where you no longer care about rejection. *Rejection* or *failure* is a reminder you're being **divinely** guided.

Day #132

Are you **checking in** with **yourself** to make sure you're on the right path? Making sure that you're going in a **direction** that feels good to you. That you're **moving** with an **intention** that you can **hono**r. Are you diving deep into our own **soul** to **find** that direction?

Day #133

READY to make your dreams a reality? Be **specific** with what you want. What does your **soul** want? What is truly in **alignment** for you? What is **truly** attainable this year and then for future years? When you are specific about it, you can **manifest** it with **ease**.

Day #134

Ask yourself what can you do? Not what can you do tomorrow, but what *can* you do *today*? What can you do right *now*? What's that one thing you can do to *break* past that *fear* optimizing and utilizing this very *moment* in time?

Day #135

WHAT you can do is **reinvent** yourself. You have a fresh **opportunity** to create yourself as you chose to be. Who do you want to be? **Knowing** what you know now with your past experiences and **bringing** in your *goals, ambitions,* and *desires.* WHO do you choose to be? **Reinvent** yourself to be that person you *imagine.*

Day #136

Are your guides **redirecting** you? Are they trying to expose you to something **new**? Are they pulling away the old layers that have kept you protected but no longer serve your highest good? Are you **listening** to them? Are you getting yourself out of the way enough to allow that guidance to come in for you?

Day #137

Sit with yourself. *Don't* sit with your friends or family. Instead, sit with your *higher self*. Your all-knowing self. Ask yourself

Who do I want to be?

Who am I meant to be?

Who am I underneath all of this?

When your higher self *whispers* back, be willing to peel away those layers you've built to be *true* to who you are *underneath* it all.

Day #138

YOU can have these little *hurdles* that serve as *tests* from the *Universe*. When it *feels* like a constant *struggle*, or you have to force it, there's something the Universe is telling you, that it's not right-the flow isn't there. The *energetic* flow is needed in order for you to have *balance* and to *manifest*. If it's a constant struggle you have to *wonder* about that.

Day #139

Trust and drift with *Spirit*.
Surrender. Get out of your way.
Show up. *Step up* and when you
do, you will begin to *see* that
path that seemed so foggy
before, that seemed so
unbelievably *difficult* to *navigate*,
opens up.

Day #140

Understand that you do have choices. You think you don't because you tell *yourself* you don't. You think there is *nothing* that you can do, when there is *always* something you can do doing. It's about getting real with yourself and not creating any *excuses*.

Day #141

Don't be afraid of new beginnings. It's **trusting** and knowing that spirit is putting you there because you are ready. **Because** in some way you have asked for it. *You have called it in*. They're not going to give it to you if you are not ready. The slate is being **cleaned** so you can **grow** in your **garden**!

Day #142

Your *intuition* is the most basic of all of the *gifts* you can *develop*. You already have it within you. That is the mechanism of your survival. *Allow* yourself to grow it, to trust it to allow it to be *your* compass in life rather than *dismissing* it.

Day #143

BE a *Soul Hunter*. That means you go into your *soul*. You go *deep* within. You're hunting for what's there. You're hunting for what needs to be *healed*. You're *hunting* for things deep within that are *unresolved* and you find that *resolution*. You're *hunting* for your *truth*.

Day #144

When you **uphold** your **boundaries,** there will be those that don't like it and may find ways to make you feel *less* than, or to make you feel **selfish** because they need that to justify their **motivation**. See them for who they are and **release** them with love. **Surround** yourself with those that **honor** you.

Day #145

As you progress and **evolve** through your **soul growth**, you will start to see how the *universe* is bringing you into new found awareness. You will experience a shift where certain **relationships** are **no longer** in alignment. This is simply due to your **vibration** rising so it's important to your soul work to honor it and hold your **boundaries**.

Day #146

Remember that you don't need closure from *another* person. *Closure* comes within. When you feel that you need it from another go within and trust your own *intuition*. *Nothing* is as *clear* as listening to your *own* intuition.

Espresso

YOURSELF

Day #147

You are *not* meant to be the same as everyone else. You are *not* a carbon copy. Let go of this idea of a perfect life. It's an *illusion*. You are designed to be unique and *bountiful* in your *own* way so that you *share* your talents and gifts with others. *Express* yourself *unapologetically* and allow your soul to *shine*.

Day #148

IF you are being stretched too thin, rest up. *Fill* your tank! Don't worry about trying to please everybody. It's *impossible* to please everyone! Do what you need to do and do what you feel is fair. Then that's it. You have to *cut the chord* with it!

Day #149

Release the baggage you carry. Consider what is *weighing* you down. Whether it be physically, mentally or energetically. *Wrap* it up and take it to the trash. Walk it to the *dumpster*. When your mind is free, your spirit is free to *manifest* and *propel* you forward.

Day #150

Success comes from being in your power. **Own** that. Be **brave** and **help** others **find** their own **path**.

Day #151

Closure comes from *forgiveness* for yourself and forgiveness for others. Not *holding* on to those feelings of expecting a different outcome. *Releasing* any desire for an apology and *finding* that peace within without *one*.

Day #152

YOU spend a lot of time and energy **consumed** by work and obligations. That's a **big** part of your life and if you're not **happy** with it then you are giving your **power** away. You're giving your power away to **support** a life that doesn't feel joyful. Find something you are **passionate** about. Find something that **ignites** you from **within**.

Day #153

Self-love is about being satisfied with who you are as a spirit being. Whether you *perceive* yourself with flaws or not, it's *recognizing* and accepting yourself as you are, not as you wish to be. It's about *finding* that truth that lies within you. That *truth* that says you're worth more than what you give yourself credit for.

Day #154

Some blocks take *longer* than others to **release**. You have to give yourself a chance. Consider how long you've been *holding* onto it for. How long did it take you to **absorb** it and push it down? That's a lot of **energy** and **effort**. It didn't build overnight, so you can't expect to **purge** it overnight. It may take a little time and compassion on your part. Your *biggest* stride is to **face** it, because once you *acknowledge* it you can fully **release** it.

Day #155

Reflect on your *past* relationships. Which ones *hurt* you the most? *Ever* been in a relationship where it *felt* like constant *struggle*? Were you constantly trying to make it *work*? Those are the *times* when you have to surrender, not force it, let it go. *Remove* the *toxicity* from your life.

Day #156

HOW many *times* have you *resisted* where spirit is *trying* to take you? You may have these *preconceived* notions of where you think you should be going and, yet, *Spirit* may have a *completely* different plan for you. When you can *drift* with *Spirit*, you will be absolutely surprised at what will *unfold* before you.

Day #157

When you take care of yourself and *nurture* your soul you are going to discover the *secret* to *manifestation*. Your dreams and aspirations will take hold and become *reality* because it all comes back to *self-love*. It all comes back to you taking care of **YOU** first.

Day #158

HOW are you treating yourself on the inside? Are you **speaking** to yourself **kindly**? Are you holding your head high with pride? If not, **practice** it. Are you letting other people **dominate** or control you? Don't allow someone else's **negativity** to be **your** truth. That is not spirit truth. Spirit would never speak **negative** words to **you**.

Day #159

Love your body. Look at yourself in the mirror and **embrace** your **physical** vessel. If you're *not* in a place where you're fully **secure** in your body, work on it without **excuses**. Without **blaming** other people. Work on achieving what it is you feel you would need to be in **alignment** with yourself. Your **higher self**.

Day #160

Feeling the emotions of another as your own is your *empathic* sense. Sometimes you may not know the difference between what yours is vs. that of another. *How* do you know? Simply ask! Ask your higher self. If it's theirs release it. If it's yours-own it. Own it and *embrace* it. Good or bad. High or low vibration. Own it so you can *navigate* and work through it.

Day #161

Settle in. Settle in to your *soul*. Meditate and say ask if you are living *authentically*? Are you living your life to your fullest *potential*? This is an opportunity for you to look at your *circumstance* so that you can make better and stronger choices for you and your *family* and *friends* moving forward.

Day #162

You are a **lightworker**. Use your energy. Use your **gift**. Remain centered and stay connected to your higher self. **Exude** your powerful light. With your **positive** energy you'll create a shift. Not a shift just for yourself, but a shift for the world. **You** have an **opportunity** to give back.

Take advantage of it.

Day #163

HOW do you stay **positive**? It's easy to fall into stress. It's easy to **feel** anxiety. How do you **stay** in alignment and connected to your higher self? **Breathe**. When that anxiety steps in take a breath. Using your breath allows the stress to move away and keep you connected to your higher self. **Believe** you are safe and trust it will all work out. Stay **positive** as it helps to **raise** the vibration.

Day #164

The more you *trust* and put yourself out there, the more you will build that *natural* relationship with spirit. When you hesitate, worry, panic, and question spirit, you will experience more bumps because you will be allowing your ego mind to attempt to *manipulate* the pure energy of spirit.

Day #165

Has **complacency** become your safety net? Have you allowed **fear** to bottle up inside of you? Perhaps, you're allowing fear to control your life to the point where you are **limiting** your own **freedom**. Limiting what you were put on this earth to do. Limiting your **purpose**. Is this how you want to keep living?

Day #166

DON'T *force* friendships. Don't try to make people *like* you. It's *wasted* energy and It will never work. The more you own who you are, the *Universe* will respond in kind. It will bring that right flow, that right *energy*, that right *opportunity* and that *right* person *directly* to you.

Day #167

It's about having **respect** for Spirit. Having respect for this beautiful **miracle** that is all around you. You are not separate from **Spirit**. The distance is only what you are **creating**, it is not coming from Spirit. You are **one** with the spirit world.

Day #168

When you can take a step back and understand that although a *dream* may be your end vision, there's a *path* for you to take. You have to *navigate* that path. Just because you take a *wrong* turn or there's a bump doesn't mean you're supposed to let go of your *dream*. You're just supposed to navigate it a little *differently*.

Day #169

NEW *beginnings* are really a wonderful way to find *fulfillment*, to find your happiness without settling. It takes *trust*, it takes a *desire* to take chances and have courage. It can feel like a challenge, but it's worth it. This is why *Spirit* is bringing it forward. Because it is a new *beginning*.

Day #170

HOW many times have you gotten a *feeling* about someone or something that just doesn't feel right, but you can't prove it? Just because it's not *proven* doesn't mean you are wrong. You have to *trust* that your gut. Your *intuition* is proof enough. Stop justifying your *instincts* and start *trusting* your gut.

Day #171

You may **question** why something is taking so long to **manifest**. Spirit is ensuring you are emotionally **prepared**. Giving you time to purge whatever needs to be released. Perhaps there's some **emotions** that need to be processed before you are ready, this is **Spirit** timing.

Day #172

YOU are trying too hard, *slow down*, look deeper, work on it, and *trust* the *divine* timing. It will happen when it's supposed to happen.

Day #173

ASK yourself about your job. Do you *enjoy* what you're doing? That's the first *question*. If you don't enjoy what you're doing, then *stop* letting fear, insecurity, and uncertainty block you from *digging* deep to find out what you truly want and *going* for it.

Day #174

You GIVE fear so much *power*.
Can you imagine what you
would *accomplish* if you stopped
giving fear your *power*?

Day #175

If it *falls* away it's meant to be, it's for your *highest* good. You don't have to hold on so *tightly* to what is no longer serving you. This may be hard to *grasp* because you want it to all work out, but it only falls into place as you *surrender*.

Day #176

You get into your patterns, stick with your habits and stay in your safety zones. When you can sit and ask Spirit

What change is in store for me? What am I supposed to be learning?

You will open the gateway. It's about learning, taking what you learn and growing from it. Allowing that change to set in.

Day #177

DO you *realize* that when you connect to your own loved one, whether that be through a *sign*, a *symbol* or through a *memory*, you are *serving* spirit? So, each and every time that happens, you are making a connection and serving *spirit*.

Day #178

Give yourself the gift of believing in yourself. You don't have to have the **confidence** immediately, just have the courage. With **experience** your confidence will start to rise up. When you **limit** yourself, you are limiting all of your capability, all of your beautiful **potential** that spirit is giving you that your **soul** knows.

Day #179

IN order to be *successful*, you need planning. You have to have that *self-discipline* to structure your next steps.

WHAT do you want to accomplish and what are your goals? Many lightworkers, say;

I don't need to do anything. The universe will bring it to me.

The universe brings it to those who *strive* for it.

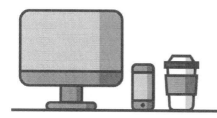

WORK HARD.
HAVE FUN.
MAKE A DIFFERENCE.

Day #180

THINK of the *greatness* that you can accomplish by *moving forward*. If you took one hour each day and took action towards that goal, look at how much *progress* you would make towards what you desire in just a week! Take *action* towards what you *desire*.

Day #181

You **create** your **reality**. So, if you *don't* like your reality. **Know** that you're the one *creating* it and you're the one who can **change** it.

Day #182

Trust in divine timing. Spirit is not going to *move* you in a direction you're not ready for and they won't give you something you can't handle. They will *present* it to you when you are in a space and place of being accepting of what is being *given* to you. That is when it will unfold. That is *divine* timing.

Day #183

Don't **compromise** on your potential because you don't **believe** in yourself enough. Release any mindset that you aren't capable of **achieving** greatness or fearful of creating waves among those you love. Spirit **nudges** you towards greatness because that is your calling. Your **destiny**.

Day #184

WHEN you are stressed, under pressure, sad or frustrated, it's very difficult to have **clear** thoughts. It's very challenging to have a clear vision of the answer. When you can **shift** your thoughts and change how you are **perceiving** something, you can then create peace and in that peace comes **clarity**.

Day #185

Want to *reach* a goal? Create a positive thought. *Visualize* it and feel it in your body. Feel the *sensation* of reaching that goal. This creates *positive energy* because you are more relaxed, feeling joyful and your vibration is rising. As you do this, you'll start to see ways on how to *achieve* your goal.

Day #186

HOW are your **relationships**? Are you happy in them? Are you feeling **fulfilled**? All relationships take *compromise*. They **require** *commitment* and *dedication*, but you shouldn't feel like you're settling. If you **feel** like you're settling, you're using **fear** to keep you in them.

Day #187

Your soul is **encompassed** by your physical body. Why do you think that is? It's so your **soul** can have a physical experience.

You **learn** lessons in your physical vessel. Yes, you work through obstacles, **overcome** disappointment and rebound from setbacks, but you also **experience** love, joy and excitement. It's all a part of your soul experience!

Day #188

Reflecting on your life, is there anything that you don't like about it? *Change it!* Don't complain about it. Do *something* about it. You have that ability. You have *free will*. You're *blessed* with the freedom to choose the life you desire, a life that *resonates* with you. One that *feels* good.

Day #189

WHEN you compare your physical life to your *entire* soul's journey, the journey from this realm to the next and beyond to reincarnation. This *specific* physical experience is a mere spec. Forgo procrastination and *maximize* your physical experience for it literally is a once in a lifetime moment for your soul.

Day #190

BE your own *best* friend. Especially when you are *feeling* run down and have too much on your plate. When you're *exhausted*, you don't have the same energy or stamina. You need to be your own best friend and *give* yourself the break you need.

Day #191

Whatever you do, whatever it is, don't let it *fear* control you. Don't let it hold you hostage for this entire physical experience, okay? Work through your stuff so you can create a clearer channel and **manifest** the life you know you want, and you know you deserve.

Day #192

HOW many times has life shifted around you? It may be unexpected. You lose your job, or a relationship, *but* it's *always* sudden. Perhaps, you experience complete *betrayal*. It feels unexpected and it hurts. This is *Spirit* letting you know there is a misalignment that *needs* to be addressed to get you on *back on track*.

Day #193

MOST people don't *realize* how imperative organization is to success. Regardless of your industry, organizing will *help* you create a plan. That plan will help to *lessen* anxiety and create peace for yourself. *Decide* what you want to call into your life and *organize* it! Want to be successful? What is your plan?

Day #194

Life becomes such a hustle and bustle that it can be dominating. Take a *moment* to stop the movement around you. *Quiet* the outside chatter and go inwards to ask your soul what it needs for *complete* happiness. *Honor* the answer you receive as it's your truth. It's your *unfiltered* truth.

Day #195

Ask yourself, what is the Universe trying to change for you? What is Spirit **bringing** to you? Is there any area in which you are resisting by saying **I don't want this change?** *Remember,* the universe is there for you and it can only help if you **allow** it. *Never* be afraid of change if it's *spirit inspired.*

Day #196

WHEN you're in your darkest moments **dig deep** and find your inner strength and **connect** with Spirit. Remember there are **brighter** days for you and your potential is so much greater than you could possibly imagine. Spirit is **always** by your side **supporting** you even during your most difficult times.

Day #197

When you begin to surrender the *magic* happens. Your purpose comes forward. Your *soul* starts to fill with joy. Your spirit begins to *dance*. Your smile returns and your aura is so glowing that people say, *What have you done to yourself?* It's not magic. It's the light and shine of spirit that *sparkles* within you.

Day #198

Soul hunting gives you an opportunity to **discover** who are you deep within. Not in your head, but in your heart. To *know* that you're **worthy** and that there is something special about you. *Because there is something **special**.* Don't allow insecurities, false people and projections cover you up. **Unveil** your light.

Day #199

Your **soul** is *all knowing.* Your soul is all **love**. You are not supposed to be going through life **feeling** afraid because your soul is like, *Are you kidding? Snap out of it! You got this! You are* **ALL-KNOWING**. *Get a grip and remember your* **magical** *powers.*

Day #200

FIND a way to be **comfortable** and fulfilled with being alone first. That's the **key**. Then you won't feel the need to have a companion to **feel** whole. To feel **loved**. You will find that within, and you will end up attracting someone who **deserves** you. This new relationship won't feel needy. If you're feeling needy, that is **fear** coming forward.

Day #201

Do *not* be afraid. When you feel tested, *rise up* and love stronger for we have *chosen* you to *represent* all that is good and all that is possible. Your heart may feel like it will break, but you are *stronger* than you believe. You are the *connection* to the Universe; the infinite is *within* you.

Day #202

ONE person is *not* more
deserving over another. Spirit is
saying, *Oh, give it to this person, but
don't give it to you.* You are meant to
have a great life and be *fulfilled*.
You are meant to be your best,
highest version and vibration of
yourself. You are *deserving*, and
Spirit wants nothing but
abundance for you.

Day #203

WHEN you're *feeling* stuck and having trouble navigating your dream, begin by *focusing* on what you want to manifest! *Don't* just expect it to happen. When you *experience* those setbacks, figure out what you need to do to push forward and move past it. *Trust* that you can get past this bump.

Day #204

IT'S about **trusting** that *feeling* that you are getting. If a thought **pops** into your head out of the blue and you **weren't** expecting it, that is your indicator, your blinking light. **Trust** that.

This is your intuition kicking in.

Day #205

Your psychic senses go FAR *beyond* your physical senses and the spirit world is so ***divinely*** intelligent that they *know* how to reach you. Even though they are *not* in a physical body, they understand how to ***tap*** into your ***senses*** to communicate.

Day #206

YOU must stand up for yourself. *Stand up* and create a life that is going to be *fulfilling* for you. Until you start speaking up, *owning* your truth and *living* authentically, you are going to be *trapped* by the egos of others. You will be because that is how they *choose* to control.

Day #207

ALLOW Spirit to be the boss and *submerse* yourself into the cadence of universal timing. Begin to *see* how life unfolds as it's supposed to, and that force is *no* longer needed. *Observe* how opportunities present themselves. Be *willing* to own where you are and be willing to *surrender* to Spirit.

Day #208

There's **no** such thing as *fearlessness*. There is fear when you're being **challenged**. There is fear when you are facing the unknown, but trust and courage can **overcome** fear. That's the concept of *fearlessness*. To say to yourself **I may be scared, but I'm going for it anyway.**

Day #209

When you're wanting that loved one in Spirit to visit you, *allow* yourself to relax. Let go of putting *pressure* on yourself to make a connection. Especially, if you're grieving. When you are grieving your vibration is lower and you need *time* to heal. Relax your body and expand your *awareness* so you can pick up on the subtleties that the *Spirit* world is giving you.

Day #210

FIND your grit and never quit. That is your **secret** to **success**. You may feel challenged and *want* to give up. **Find** your grit when this happens. By **showing** up for yourself, you will **continue** to make progress.

Each and **every** time you say **yes**, you *move* forward.

Day #211

Sometimes those blocks you experience are **given** to you as a **gift**. They are given to prove to you that you can **overcome** that obstacle. You are then able to **help** others with that specific issue.

Day #212

WHEN you *can't* see the light at the end of the tunnel. *Stop* focusing on the end of the tunnel. Just *focus* on the next step instead. Don't try to *conquer* it all at once. *Let go* of focusing on the big picture. Just take a look to see what *needs* to be done in this *moment*.

Day #213

When you FEEL that your back is against the wall, have **faith**. Be resilient. It's a reminder to your soul that maybe it's just about **needing** a little *more* faith to get you **through** this.

Day #214

Your **truth** comes from your heart. Your truth comes from your soul. Your truth comes from that inner **knowing** and your **higher** self. When you are in tune with that, you are **living** in your truth. Your truth is then very easy to see, feel, hear, and know. You'll be living in an **organic** place of authenticity. A place where you are no longer afraid to **speak** your truth.

Day #215

YOU may chase a **dream**, chase a relationship, chase a friendship or a job. You may find yourself **constantly** chasing. Do you find yourself **forcing** something that maybe isn't right? When you keep chasing, you're **wasting** energy. You'll always be one step behind. Instead of chasing. How about **embracing**?

Day #216

There are times in your life where you get stuck. *Maybe* you're *stuck* in the past or in a current situation. Your mind chatter takes over. *Self-doubt* steps in. You may feel ready to move ahead, but you're afraid of making the *wrong* decision, so you refuse to make *any* decision. Work past the paralysis, make a decision and *trust* in yourself.

Day #217

WHEN you're in your *truth*, you're going to *feel* more *powerful* than you ever have felt before because you will be *centered*, *grounded* and *connected*. When you are truly *connected* no one can throw you off your path. *No One*.

Day #218

Trust and let go of the *need* to be right or to *feel* as if you have to make this perfect *choice*. Instead, simply honor

This is the choice I'm being led to. That will really help you *release* the pressure that you're putting on yourself and you'll see where the *Universe* is *leading* you.

Day #219

STOP comparing yourself to another. *No more* second guessing your path. *Everyone* has their own unique journey. Their *life* lessons. Look at yourself. What do *you* need for *happiness*? What do you need for fulfillment? If you *waste* your time focusing on another, you are depriving your *soul* of *discovery* and opportunity.

Day #220

Sometimes you get hurt and you're in so much pain it can make you *feel* stuck. *Pain* is part of life and its part of your *experience*. You are *not* meant to stay in it. The Universe, Spirit, your guides do *NOT* want you to stay in the pain. The pain is merely a *lesson*. You learn from it. You *grow* from it and it creates your *story*.

Day #221

As an **empath** you *feel* the emotions of another. You will feel them as your very own. You will tend to be very **emotional**. This is part of your *soul contract*. **When** your **heart** hurts or when you are feeling sad, check in with yourself.

Is this my emotion or someone else's? If it belongs to another return it with **love** so that you are protecting your energy and maintaining balance.

Day #222

KNOW that when you *step* into the *power* of love, you are the almighty powerful. WHEN you *remember* that you are all one you become one. When one is wounded. *All* are wounded. When one is healed. All are *healed*. And when one is loved. All are *loved*.

Day #223

The more you can **stand** in your **power** with your light, truth, honesty and integrity, the more it's going to **resonate** with those who need you the most. You're also going to **pull** in the support system you need. That **foundation** helps you to **build** the relationships in your life that truly means something.

Day #224

YOUR soul is your **unique** fingerprint. It's your mark of **essence**. This is *your* gift, *your* light to the world. Allowing your soul to **shine** is honoring this **beautiful** gift from Spirit and the Universe. There is NO other **you** as Spirit calls on **you** to rise up and **shine** the light for others.

happy moment

Day #225

THERE comes a moment when you have to *listen* to your soul's whisper. Your soul's *whisper* is that *little voice* deep within that tells you that there's something more. You're meant for something *greater*. Whatever it is for you, take a moment and *listen* to your *soul's* whisper. It's never wrong and it's time to stop playing it *safe*.

Day #226

WHEN you are *focused* on your path and discern where you *place* your energy and *clear* on your purpose, the universe and spirit will bring people and *opportunities* to you. They will put you in specific situations to help you *manifest* your dreams and goals.

Day #227

IF you're spending time with someone and it's **no** longer **feeling** rewarding or fulfilling, then maybe you have to **reconsider** that relationship or look at how you're **spending** your time with that person. Not everyone **deserves** your energy. If they don't then it's time to let them **go** and **move** on.

Day #228

WHEN you stand in your *power* it's **amazing** how Spirit works. It's like dancing in the *rhythm* of the Universe. It's this pure vein and **natural** flow. You'll just find yourself moving and **swaying** to the sound of Spirit. When you stay in that rhythm and keep **listening**, you will grow, **blossom** and you will find yourself dancing with Spirit.

Day #229

WHEN you *deal* with a narcissist it can be so painful because they will actually *purposely* try to hurt you. If you're a sensitive, and you're *empathetic*, this is going to hurt even more. Create and *honor* your boundaries so they can't get to you. Deny your desire to '*love them enough*' for they can only have love for *themselves*.

Day #230

You get this **one** physical life and this one unique **experience**. Why not go for what you've always dreamt of doing? Many people **expect** that it will just show up, it will just be there, it will just **manifest**. That's not the case. It takes a lot of **work**. It takes a lot of dedication. It takes a lot of commitment. But it also takes your **dream**.

Day #231

COULD your **physical** pain have an emotional tie? There are times in which **emotional** baggage, unresolved blocks or past life experiences disguise themselves as a physical **ailment**. It may be an indicator that you are **holding** onto something that is creating a physical ailment in your body. **Ask** if there is **anything** that needs *healing* and *releasing*.

Day #232

STOP being a *people pleaser*. The person who always wants to 'fix' *everything* and is afraid to say **NO**. Guess what happens to *you*? You fall right down your priority list. You put yourself LAST and you fail to take care of your needs first. No self-care, no self-love. It's time for **YOU**! Start exercising your boundaries and practicing the word *no* for your own well-being!

Day #233

Why are you putting **all** of your dreams, goals and aspirations on the **back burner**? You have this opportunity to **stand up** and do something by creating a life that you truly desire. STOP hitting that snooze button. **Get up** earlier. **Plan** your day. What are you waiting for?

Day #234

YOUR energy is **contagious**. By using your connection with the divine to **raise** your vibration, you are also raising the **vibration** for others. Those around you will begin to **feel** more energetic, joyful, and optimistic. EVEN in dark or uncertain times you are a light for others.

Day #235

Negative thoughts have so much energy. It's easy to become *obsessive* about a negative thought. It will repeat itself over and over in your head. *Shift* your thoughts. Replace your negative thought with a *positive* one. See how it begins to unfold exactly how it's meant to be. The universe has a *beautiful* system in place when you *trust* it.

Day #236

Are you *focusing* on the end result, rather than focusing on your *next* step? This may *feel* overwhelming and discouraging. Instead, ask

What is my next best step?

Then, let go of control and put your *focus* on the next *step* to achieve your goal.

Day #237

PAIN is a part of *life*. It's part of your experience. You're *not* meant to *stay* in pain. The Universe, spirits and your guides, don't want you to stay in the *pain*. They want you to *feel* love. The pain is an experience. You *learn* from it and grow from it. Sometimes, there is no *rhyme* or particular *reason* for it.

The pain is an overall *experience*.

Day #238

LOOK at where you're **stuck** and know you don't have to stay there. **You** can make a choice to move out of it. It's a **conscious** choice. You won't be able to wave a **magic** wand because you have to do the work. You have to make the **commitment**. You have to roll up your sleeves, and **dive** in, but it's absolutely possible!

Day #239

Don't **give** energy in the **direction** you are **not** going. Let go of the feeling that you have to **respond** to people, situations, or drama that doesn't feel good. **Period.**

End of story. You don't have to **apologize**. NO need to feel guilty. You don't have to sit there and justify yourself. **Honor your path**.

Day #240

TAKE a *moment* today and really honor one of your loved ones in Spirit. *Take* yourself through a memory. Feel their *presence* with you. WHEN they're giving you a sign or symbol, acknowledge it. That's *how* you can honor and remember them. That's how you show them you *believe* they are still with you.

Day #241

You can **build** your intuition with practice. By using your **intuition** every day, it becomes stronger. It's **literally** a connection between your **physical** body and your **higher** self. By connecting these two, your body becomes an **intuitive** compass that you can use to make decisions. **Continue** to *build* it, and it will become so much more **natural** for you.

Day #242

Stop *letting* fear hold you back. Do not give fear your power. Your power *deserves* more. *Give* love your power. Give courage your power. Give faith your power. Give hope your *power* and have *faith* in yourself, you can do it.

Day #243

Your soul *lives* on. It's only the physical body you no longer need. Spirit *continuously* gives you these gifts each and every day. These messages to connect and *communicate* with you. Whether it's seeing a hummingbird, making you think of your grandmother or hearing your dad's favorite song on the radio or your guides *giving* you that sign you *asked* them for. They are constantly showing up for you.

Day #244

IS the **direction** that you are moving in alignment with your **soul's** purpose? At the end of the day if you keep **plugging** along and not **listening** to your soul or not being true to your **higher self**, you will feel unfulfilled. *Like something is missing.* IF you get this feeling, ask your soul

What are you needing?

Listen to your soul's response.

Day #245

Rather than *looking* outside to *bring* it in, *start* INSIDE and *pull* it OUT!

Day #246

WHEN you **hear** that little voice and feel that **nudge** of inspiration and a thought pops in to say;

There's something more for you.
YES, there *is* something more for you. If you are hearing that, feeling that seeing that, TRUST that there is something *more* for you.

Day #247

The DEAL is, you've got a *destiny*. You have a life purpose! Yes, *you* do! You might as well get *started* on it.

Day #248

It STARTS with **believing** in you. Stop trying to fit into the **mold** of what others think you should be and **embrace** who you are on the inside. BE your most **authentic** self and love that self. WHEN you love you, *all of you*, even the stuff that you may struggle with the most, you will emit **more** energy, positivity and love out to the world.

Day #249

You have to **remember** that you can all **grow** and **evolve**, but don't be a hater on yourself, okay? There are enough haters out in the world!

Be a lover of yourself.

Be a *lover* of *you!*

Day #250

You are *intuitive*. It's your fight or flight response. When you can understand it and *expand* your *awareness* you will pick up on energy. You may *see* it. You may *feel* it. You may simply *know* it. It's just that overall *sense* which may not make *logical* sense, but it's your gut talking to you.

Trust that conversation.

Day #251

YOU can *only* be disappointed when you *create* a perceived outcome or response. *Life* is about *living*. Life is about creating, loving, and *staying* PRESENT in the moment. There is *no* disappointment in *mindfulness*.

Day #252

A **narcissist** will **flip** and **distort** the truth, but remember, in **their** mind, it IS the truth. In their mind they have somehow absolutely **convinced** themselves this is the golden **truth**. Your self-love, self-confidence and boundaries are your **best** defense against a narcissist.

Day #253

Allowing your soul to shine is
honoring this *beautiful* gift that
you've been given from *Spirit*.
SHINE it for yourself and *shine*
it for SPIRIT.

Day #254

You are **perfect** in your imperfections! You have to ask yourself if they are even **imperfections** at all? Maybe your traits are what **help** you contribute to society as a whole. Perhaps, YOU are what is needed, and you just haven't accepted it. **Embrace** ALL of you. The good, the bad and the unknown.

Day #255

You're going to have **struggles**; you're **going** to have doubts and even insecurities. This is **completely** natural. Rather than allowing those thoughts and feelings to **dominant** your mind, simply acknowledge with

I love me! I am lovable. I am worthy. You are not welcomed here.

Wash away *any* negativity with positivity.

Day #256

WHEN you have an idea, whether it be a feeling, vision or concept, *believe in it*! Believe in your power to manifest! You are so deserving, but *how* many times have you told yourself that you are not?

You have to *believe* in yourself and when you do, your thoughts, feelings and visions become *reality*.

Day #257

How many *times* have you had an *experience* and **dismissed** it? How many times have you **interacted** with a person and your intuition told you to *walk away* because something doesn't feel right? The more you **trust** that it's your own safety system, your own *GPS*, your own compass, the easier it is to **navigate** your life.

Day #258

Ask yourself every morning if you are you *fully* surrendering or are you holding yourself back? Are you getting in *your* own way? It is about trust, and trusting spirit, to know that you are in *good* hands.

Day #259

WE are all *pieces* to a *puzzle*.
Know that it's OK if you are still
searching for your piece.

How do you fit in?

It's finding where you are and
letting go of needing validation
and *trusting* that you *do* fit in.
Know that you are needed to
make the universal puzzle
complete. It can *never* be complete
with YOU in it.

Day #260

Spirit is the answer. Spirit wants to be *acknowledged*. Sprit wants you to know they are with you. They want *you* to *know* they are around, and they want you to *trust* them. They want to *ease* your fear and for you to not be worried and to *never* doubt their presence.

Day #261

HOW many *times* have you been told it's all in your head or that you are *making* things up? Maybe you've been told that it's your *imagination* getting the best of you. Those who *discount* you have something to hide. They are *hiding* from the truth. Trust your intuition as it's the *language* of truth.

Day #262

Believe in you! It's pretty simple when you think about it! *Don't* complicate it by *giving* your self-worth away or giving your lovability away. Those are the *qualities* to value the most within yourself as others will take them for *granted* without thinking twice!

Day #263

We see you *looking* for signs or symbols to guide you. Those signs, those symbols, must *start* from *within*. Believing in yourself, in your core in what you want, and finding *clarity* with that, through quietness. It's through the mindfulness and the *presentness* that you find the meaning of those signs and symbols that we *give* you.

Day #264

Do not *forget* your own light. Do
not burn out your *candle*. You
are meant to keep it lit to *show*
the way for others. Remember
that no matter what you've been
through, it's sincerely meant to
prepare you for where you are
and meant to put you in the
world to help others to rise
beyond their setbacks.

Day #265

WHEN you are feeling stretched too thin, *remember* you are *not* a rubber band. If you keep *stretching* you *will* break. *Give* yourself the and self-care you need so that you *don't* stretch yourself to your *breaking* point.

Day #266

YOU have the **energy** to **spread** love for all and we ask that in these times of uncertainty you cast away your **fears**, judgements and uncertainties to help spread the **message** of love. We ask that you spread your **love** to as many corners of the world to **raise** the vibration of all. You are a **vessel**.

A *messenger* of love.

Day #267

DON'T get so **locked** into what you *HAVE been doing* to **limit** yourself as to what you CAN be **doing** in this moment to expand **yourself**.

Day #268

WHEN you *really* trust and **own** your worth, you are seen, you are heard, and the Universe will **respond**.

Just ONE caveat:

It MUST to be in **alignment** with your *higher self* and in **alignment** with your *soul*.

Day #269

Remember, it's about *loving* yourself. Loving yourself enough to *remove* negative thoughts, negative people, *and* negative situations from your life. To be *bold* and *courageous* in doing so.

Day #270

IF you are surrounded by people who you *don't* support you, *find* *new* people.

Your people *should* want to *see* you *succeed*. Your people should be clapping when you get a raise, promotion, fall in love or find success. They should be *clapping* for you.

If they aren't. *Run*. Run Fast.

Day #271

Avoid **comparing** yourself to another. When YOU compare yourself, you are going to feel **less than** or you are going to quantify your level of success based on what someone **else's** IDEAS and ACTIONS.

That's never going to get you in **alignment** with where **you're** supposed to be.

Day #272

WHEN you get an *intuitive* hit of some kind find a way to say it out loud. *Find* a way to *listen* to your intuition *without* judgement. LISTEN to what you are being given. *Honor* it. *Don't* dismiss it. We tend to dismiss it way too much.

Day #273

TODAY we *smile* at you and wrap our arms around you and wait ***patiently*** while you ***discover*** how *magnificently* wonderful you are in EVERY way.

Day #274

DON'T worry about *other* people. Just know you've only got *one* boss, and that *boss* is SOURCE.

Day #275

You ***don't*** have to ***hold*** onto hurt. You don't have to hold onto the ***pain*** that someone has caused you. You don't have to hold onto the ***negativity*** that you feel from another. That's ***not*** yours to hold onto. If you hold on to everyone's ***projections*** it will only ***weigh*** you down.

You don't have to worry about it, let ***source*** handle it.

Day #276

There are *times* when we ask you sit alone. To *sit* with your thoughts and feelings. To look inward and upward as you *reunite* with your *source* power. The power of us that resides *within* you. This *power* serves as a reminder that *all* is *possible*, and all is ready for you as you *accept* it with love and grace.

Day #277

We *create* opportunities for you to connect with others. A connection that is *pure* and rare as *within* each of you remembers the neighbor next to you. A *love* and *bond* that is deeper than your physical form. A *connection*, as you look around, that tells you that are *not* alone. You have others to love and support you.

Day #278

SPEND time in *nature*. Spend *time* with trees, smelling the air, and grounding to the earth. When you do that, you *allow* yourself to *reconnect* with nature and the elements around you. By connecting to nature, you connect with *spirit*. You're connecting to that higher *vibration* that is around you and within *you*.

Day #279

Why do *you* go through *life* feeling guilty? When you want to do something for yourself or take time off, you feel *guilty*. Just *give* yourself permission. When you *prioritize* yourself, by default, you prioritize everyone else around you therefore, *raising* the vibration.

It raises the bar for *everyone* and their *experience*.

Day #280

You are **meant** to experience emotions, grief and heartache to ultimately **show** you how **resilient** you are. Above it all, **you** are meant *to* **love**.

Day #281

FILL the world with your *light*.
Fill the world with your *love*.

WITH each person you *touch*,
you *serve* us.

EVERY person will be *forever*
changed by your *presence* and
your energy.

Day #282

Walk your walk, *Talk* your talk and *Stand* in your power! *Feel* good about the *actions* you are *taking* and the *decisions* you are making. At the end of the day, *check in* with *source;*

Am I in alignment with you? Am I walking the path you set forth for me?

Day #283

We will **always** lay the road of **opportunity** before you. **However,** you must remember that there is **always** a choice in **which** path you take. If you allow your **fear** to **dictate** the road upon which you take, you will **stumble,** and you will find yourself lost along the way. **Follow** us with trust as we **lead** you down the path of **living** in your purpose.

Day #284

GRATITUDE is what we ask of you. To sit and reflect.

Regardless of your circumstances, have a **sense** of gratitude for each experience as it was **intended** to help you grow. We want you to **grow**.

To **push** your *physical* and *spiritual* limits so that you can truly **blossom** into your **greatest** possible self.

Day #285

Change is here. Change comes from the *universe*. It comes from spirit. It comes from your *soul growth*.

If you can **embrace** that change, you'll actually learn so much more. You'll **learn** to *trust* and *surrender* to the *universe*.

Day #286

ASK yourself *where* can you *adjust*? In what area does your life need a bit of *calibration* so that you can feel whole? *Where* are you feeling unappreciated? *Unloved*? What is *needed* so you can feel happy, content, joy? *Don't* miss out on relishing the *joyfulness* that life has in store for *you*.

Day #287

DO you *feel* balanced? Are you getting the **intimacy** you **crave** within friendships and relationships? Is your mind, body and spirit in **alignment**?

If you answer **no** to any of these, look at what areas *feel* off so you can **adjust** and strive for *total* **balance**.

Day #288

LET GO of your *pain*.

RELEASE your *expectations*. *Fly* and soar for you are made of *greatness*.

You are a powerful being with limitless *potential*.

Day #289

We **don't** connect two people to shut them down. We **connect** two people so that they can **grow**, expand, find their **next** lesson. We **keep** some of you together, we pull some of you apart, but always **remember**, that we do this always with **purpose**.
You may not know our reason.
Trust. Trust us.

Keep an open **heart**.

Day #290

DON'T allow *yourself* to get caught up in the daily dramas of life. They are *not* what your existence is about. *Avoid* speaking *negative* words or *gossip*. They are not what your existence is about. *Speak* the words of love, openness, *acceptance* and kindness. *Live* your life with joy, for this is what your *existence* is about.

Day #291

How many *times* has spirit *not* made someone available to you? Either they're not there or they *cancel* last minute on you? Perhaps, they make *false* promises. This is sprit saying, *This is NOT your person.*

Stop making excuses for them. If Spirit *realizes* you deserve more, then believe that you do *deserve* more. You are *never* meant to CHASE someone.

Day #292

Are you *finding* the miracle in *each* day? Do you take *time* to see the *potential* that lays before you or are you blindly walking through taking it *all* for *granted*? Each day we *give* you is a blessing. It is an *opportunity* for you to feed your infinite soul. *Fill* that day with love, kindness and expression.

Day #293

TAKE a moment to *stand* in the sunlight with arms outstretched and *feel* the beauty and energy of the day we've *given* to you.

Go for a walk, spend time with family and friends and *submerse* yourself in the *gratitude* of life.

Day #294

You are **stronger** than you **believe**.
The tests you **endure** throughout
this physical life are not meant
to show you weakness, but to
show you your **strength**. When you
overcome obstacles, you **become**
stronger. You are strong enough
to **endure**, to **rise up** and to
overcome.

Day #295

Love is a *journey* of the human spirit. Love is a *path* to *connect* with higher self and others. It is *communication*. Open your heart to allow for the *greatest* experiences possible for love is the *answer* to *every* problem you could ever *imagine*.

Day #296

Remember you are **deserving** of love. Deserving of kindness, of respect and **most** of all, deserving of your destiny. Do **not** limit your **destiny** based on your **fear**.

Do not allow the little moments to take over the big picture.

When you doubt us, close your eyes and **feel** us around you and remember you are **mightier** than your current circumstances.

Day #297

IF you *stay* stuck in the *past*, you are only going to attract *more* of the past. You have already learned those lessons so *focus* forward and *trust* that if any *person* or *situation* is in the *past*, they all *deserve* to *stay* in the past!

Day #298

Having a friend, loved one or pet cross over is *never* an easy *experience* for you, *but* when a *soul* crosses, they have completed their earthbound *duties* and must *continue* on their journey. *Remember* they are *not* gone. They are *now* with us, their *Spirit* family.

Day #299

WE have *not* set you up for failure. There is *no* failure. There is only learning and *love*. With *each* moment you surrender, you *give* to the *feeling* of love again. When it seems like you *cannot* survive another day, this is when you *must* go inwards to your soul to see your *true* strength.

Day #300

Today, look for *signs* from your loved ones in Spirit, for we will *ask* them to *give* you signs today as a *celebration* of who they were in the physical and a *reminder* for you to be *present* in who *you* are today.

Day #301

IF you **purge**, your soul will **get** clear. Your soul will **feel** fresh, anew. You'll end up feeling optimistic because you are **going** to **release** all that pain, hurt, disappointment, rejection, and betrayal. You are going to **release** all the **times** you cried over someone not honoring you the way you **deserve**. You're going to **release** it all and **feel** lighter.

Day #302

OPEN your *heart* to find *forgiveness* even for the most seemingly *unforgivable* acts. For anger and hate are the *creators* of destruction. BE the *builders* of hope.

Day #303

Take **control** of your life. *Take* control of your present and your future. *Be* the inspiration that *you* need. Stop **looking** outside of yourself for validation. *When* you *find* yourself **connected** to that and in alignment, you'll *see* that you're *invincible*.

You'll see that you can create this **beautiful** life of **love**.

Day #304

Know that we come here **today** to remind you of **your** power. **Remind** you of your **glory**. Remind you that we are with you in the **power** of all that is, all that may be and all that is within you.

Together you can **create** a love so strong and so powerful that it **transitions** energy to a vibration of **unimaginable** peace and comfort.

Day #305

There is such a ***pure*** joy when you are living in ***your*** truth. When you're living your ***dream*** and ***holding*** that souls whisper in your ***heart***.

Day #306

WHAT is your *soul* saying to you? *Take* a moment and quietly listen. What does it *show* you? Are *you* getting little signs of something? *Are* you *feeling* that nudge? It may feel scary, but it's also exciting, inspiring, and fun!

Follow your soul.

Day #307

When you are able to **face** your worst-case scenario with **bravery** and surrender to the outcome, it **gives** you power.

It will feel **empowering** to be very clear on what you want because it **removes** the **fear** that blocks you.

Day #308

Remember back to *yourself*.
Remember that *you* are the *source*
of all love. Your light and love
are *your* gifts to the universe.
These are the *gifts* we *gave* to you
as a way of reminding others of
the importance of
understanding, patience,
kindness and forgiveness. *You*
have the *power* to change lives.

Day #309

Surrendering and believing is really your *first* step. *Allowing* your awareness to expand. *Connecting* the dots of the *many* little miracles around you and simply *trusting* that your loved ones are absolutely *with* you. When *you* feel those goosebumps know that is the *Spirit* realm coming *closer*.

Day #310

You **look** to others for **your** own validation, peace and approval. **Know** that all of the trust and worthiness you **seek** is already within you. You are already a **complete** package to everything you **need** to have total **fulfillment**. There is **nothing** external you need to enhance **your** experience.

Day #311

ONCE you can *see* the light *within* you. The light that *we* see. The light that we *created*.

The *light* that we *illuminate*. Then *you* will begin to *see* who you truly are with no layers *built* upon it. With *your* soul exposed you will look into the *mirror* with nothing but *love* for yourself.

Day #312

Don't lose the **freedom** of having **your** voice because you're trying to make **other** people happy. You are meant to have a **strong** voice.

One that speaks of love and self-care. A voice that **owns your** thoughts and feelings and isn't afraid to **express** itself.

Day #313

STOP hitting the *snooze* button. You *don't* get that time back. Make the most of it this point *moving* forward. *No* more *fears* worry or excuses. Stop comparing yourself. It's about rising up, *standing* in *your* power, stepping into your purpose and saying,

I'm taking my life back and I'm going to manifest all the things I desire.
No more snooze.

Day #314

YOU will **always** have human experiences that *question* your faith, *test* your beliefs and *threaten* your path, **but** trust and **know** that you were **born** for this path. You are MEANT for this path. **Allow** yourself to **trust** and take **flight**.

Day #315

It's about *finding* those ways to maintain your **strength** through your experiences. *Your* experiences make you *stronger*! You may feel **shattered** in the moment, or insecure but you have to **work** through them as **Spirit** has so much more in store for you on the **other** side of them.

Day #316

The *source* you *seek* is the source already *within* you. Trust that you are the *channeled* source.

Day #317

EVEN in your *own* life, when you *encounter* disappointments, have set-backs, experience personal *tragedies*, you can *rebuild*.

YOU can *grow*.

You can continue to *shine* your light even in the darkest of *times*.

Day #318

What is a *soul assignment*? A soul assignment is something your soul *needs* to experience in this physical lifetime. Some may call it a *life lesson*. You will *know* it's a soul assignment because it keeps *nudging* you. It may be a thought or feeling that you tuck away, *but* it will *continuously* resurface. This is when you know it is a soul assignment and you are *going* to have to *roll up* your sleeves and just do it.

Day #319

Heal the past and *let* it go. Find a place *within* yourself to understand that there was a *higher* purpose or *spirit* stepped in and maybe your soul *wanted* more. There's so many factors in this, and you can't just focus *one* thing, it's about looking at everything, *including* yourself.

Day #320

Allowing your *soul* to shine is *honoring* this *beautiful* gift that you've been given by *Spirit*.

Day #321

There's a lot in your life *where* you may *feel* unfulfilled. It can be changed! That's the *beautiful* part. You can *change* it, but you have to have the courage to *tune* in. You have to *look* inwards, and to be *honest* with *yourself*.

Day #322

Who are you *meant* to be under all of the layers you created? Be *vulnerable* in *peeling* away the layers of protection to *expose* who you truly are underneath of it all. That is *your* higher-self waiting to be *revealed*.

Day #323

Happiness lies within. Your happiness is ***not*** coming because it's already here. Let go of ***searching*** outside of yourself for love, validation and approval.

It is from ***within*** that you will ***feel*** all of the love and ***support*** we give to ***you***.

Day #324

YOU are *greatly* needed to *share* your love, *beauty*, gifts and kindness. You are *exactly* what is *needed* today and *every* day to *inspire* others.

Day #325

Our light is **your** light. Your **light** is our light. If you ever **feel** lost or your light **begins** to flicker and you find yourself in darkness, simply **look** around you and see that glow that **emanates** all around you. You are part of this **glow**. You are **one** with the light so you may always **find** your way **back** home.

Day #326

Each day you are *given* an opportunity to *serve* Spirit. It could be as simple as *extending* a kind gesture to a stranger or *helping* a friend in need. Serving Spirit is about *raising* the vibration and being a messenger *through* love, care and kindness.

Day #327

If you *slow* your breath, you will begin to *see* the gems of joy that we are giving you each and every day.

Day #328

Spirit is about *love*, KINDNESS and *giving*. Although there are times that we may be *testing* you, we are GIVING you an *opportunity* to be the *true* essence of who *you* are.

Day #329

HOW many *times* do you allow the distractions of others pull you out of your *vibration*? They either *manipulate* or attempt to make you feel guilty because you're *trying* to do something for yourself. The *solution* is to simply not give them the *energy* and the attention. Hold your *boundaries* and *honor* your vibration.

Day #330

See those goosebumps! *Feel* the hair on the back of your neck stand up. *Sense* the *energy* around you? That's YOU having a *Spirit* experience.

Day #331

WHEN is the *last* time you *pushed* the limits and let go of what is *holding* you back? When you compromise your potential, you are *limiting* your own soul and the only way there is *true* fulfillment is to surrender and trust that your potential is *limitless*. The limits are what you *create*.

Day #332

You have *freewill* to change *who* and what you are allowing in your life. *Owning* what you want and being true to *yourself*. Many *changes* will happen when you are truly owning who *you* are, but the *more* you are in your *truth* and in that *soul* space the *happier* you are going to *be*.

Day #333

When you feel *down* and *discouraged*. We want *you* to know that you are *enough*. There is *no* change to make you *greater,* for your greatness already resides *within* you.

Day #334

WHEN you look at *life* as an *opportunity* and see it as this great big road map laid before you where *nothing* is *impossible*, you will *start* to have so much more fun *living*!

Day #335

Just **breathe** and **raise** your vibration. *Trust* your team. *Trust* your path. **Do** YOU and you're going to naturally **attract** those who **support** you.

Day #336

You are **not** limited in your **potential** for all that you **dream** to be is already within you. It has **already** happened. Each time you say 'yes' to our **nudge**, you are **saying** 'yes' to your soul, your spirit and **your** light. With every *'yes'* your light **expands** and **pulsates** serving as a blanket of hope for **all** of those **around** you.

Day #337

There's an **awareness** that you have that does not come from your **conscious** mind.

It's **Spirit** saying;

I'm giving you a hug and those goosebumps, that's me applauding you. That bird you see, song you hear, penny you find or rainbow that popped up...that is also me.

This is the **miracle** of the spirit world.

Day #338

You will be *given* tests and obstacles; you are *meant* to rise above and love *beyond* them. They are *not* intended to *take* the love *out* of you.

Day #339

DO you *see* how your *fear* blocks your **abundance** of money? Perhaps you are **working** too hard. Take the breaks you need, and the money will come. *Remove* the **blocks** and it will be even **more** than *you* can imagine.

Day #340

Ready to **change** your path?
Consider what you enjoy doing
naturally every day. **Nothing** is
better than a hobby becoming a
profession if you're **passionate**
enough about it. When you
embark on a new path, know
that it will unfold as you go
along. This is the **evolution** of
your *life purpose*.

Day #341

Your *inner* compass **always** knows the way and within the state of your **confusion** there is a wonderful opportunity to *explore* new places within your soul. It is only through your perceived *limits* you begin to see the potential of *your* soul.

Day #342

YOU are *going* to take some chances here. It's *your* time to *live* in your truth. Work past your own *fear*. Remove your security blanket. *Be smart*. So, build, build, build and take these *chances* as you do it.

Day #343

We have *created* the energy of love to be so strong that it can *never* be broken. *Love* may shift, it may move, but it will *never* subside. *Your* love is our love. Our love is *always* with you. *Never* hidden, never lost. You are loved *unconditionally*.

Day #344

As you walk *through* life, **don't** be afraid to hold a hand, **give** a hug or **share** a laugh. Your connection is your **soul's** way of **reminding** you that you are **one**.

Day #345

WHEN you *doubt*, when *you* question, know that we *understand*. In your darkest space, we *encourage* you to find the inner strength to love *greater* than you ever have before. To *shine* your brightest, for love is the most *healing* tool we have *given* you to share.

Day #346

Everything is a story. When you look at your *life*, your patterns, your habits, and your *belief* systems, they are *all* systems and beliefs that you're *telling* yourself. It's the *story* that you are telling yourself.
What story are *you* holding on to that *doesn't* serve your highest good? *Release* it.

Day #347

You **want** it all now and tend to get frustrated when it isn't happening as **quickly** as you would like. This is your ego voice, **but** only when you *begin* to surrender does the **Universe** open up to **show** you the path. Allow it to unfold **naturally** and your **destiny** will reveal itself.

Day #348

You *search* to find *meaning*, your path, your purpose. Your *purpose* is to simply be you. *Be* accepting of who you already are and be *forgiving* of what *you* think you should be.
There is no becoming.
There is only *embracing*.

Day #349

The *time* is now to *start* what you have been putting off. *Build* what was *destroyed* and LOVE what has been *broken*. Mend your *heart* with love. *Reach* for your dreams, make choices that *create* freedom for your *soul*. Take *action* for now is *your* time.

Day #350

Never diminish *your* capacity to *love* and your *capacity* to give and your capacity to *shine*.

Day #351

DON'T get so **locked** into what you've *been doing* to **limit** yourself, as to what, **you** *are* **destined** *to be doing*.

Day #352

The *road* is open and laid before you. You can **take** any turn you wish. Perhaps, a long **drive** that allows you to **release** all that you **hold** onto is needed most. Take the drive. **Take** the turns and take the opportunities. **Allow** the fear to fall away and feel the **wind** on your face as you take back your **power**.

Day #353

BE BOLD enough to try something *new*. PUT your *fear* aside and *give* yourself a chance. This is *your* time to manifest. *You* are NOT limited.

Day #354

Fear is the place you **retreat** when you **lack** trust. In these **times** of uncertainty, you **forget** that we are among you. We **stand** firmly with you and even when you are unable to **feel** us in these moments, the act of **trusting** will help **you** through the dark, the *unknown* and the *unsettled*.

Day #355

We gave you *limitless* imagination so that you may have the *power* to *manifest* anything you perceive to be *possible*.

Day #356

Ask yourself what *you* are still holding on to that needs to be *released* and why are you struggling to release and heal it. Tune in to *see* what you can do to move yourself *forward*, because it's not serving your highest good to sit with it in the past. *Give* yourself the opportunity, the chance, to *let* it go!

Day #357

You **carry** so much hurt, pain and responsibility with you and you **attempt** to do this **alone**. We ask that you unload this **burden** onto us. **Sit** with us, talk to us and leave your **worries** with **us**.

Day #358

Whatever it is, find that courage to say, **I am going to embrace the change**. When you look at change as an **opportunity** with excitement and positivity, you're going to **feel** better **immediately**. When you're excited, you are *simultaneously* raising your **vibration**.

Day #359

AS you *dance* among the holiday energy, *sprinkle* your *love* everywhere. There are many *feeling* lost and lonely at this particular time of the year. *Share* your hugs and *offer* kindness at *every* turn and graciously share your *gift*.

Day #360

These **changes** and **transitions** you are experiencing are **allowing** you to **shed** the layers of the old to bring you closer into **alignment** with your soul's purpose.

Marinate in all of your **glory**.

Day #361

Are you *living* your purpose? Are you doing *everything* you can within your own power to make the *most* of your experience? Are you *maximizing* your potential in this physical experience? Remember to *always* find the *silver lining* to help you take those baby steps.

Day #362

WHEN you feel *defeated* do *not* sit down upon yourself with pity, focus on the *power* of your *soul* and your gift to rise up and *stand* in your *greatness*.

Day #363

Others who *choose* to spread negativity will also *attempt* to *discount* your light. They may place doubt upon your *dreams* and attempt to *dismantle* your power. Remember you are *stronger* than the *negative* energy they exude.

Day #364

WE see the **miracle** that we call you. It's now **your** time to **gather** your light, your **strength** and your **love** and create a **ripple** throughout the world. To be a **symbol** of hope and inspiration for others and to **remind** them there is so much to be grateful for in this **physical** experience.

Day #365

It's a *new* day, it's a new *dawn*. YOU have survived *365* days. Some of these days may been more difficult than others, but you *survived* and *thrived*. Be proud of your efforts. We now ask that you *sit* with us to *reflect* on this past year and see your growth as we do and to set your intention on what you wish to manifest in the new year. *You* have a new *beginning* just ahead of YOU.

Conclusion

There is no limit to how many times you can use this book. When you feel inspired, randomly pull a message for yourself or a friend! This is a resource that is intended to be used repeatedly, and not just for 365 days; it can be recycled year after year!

The Universe wants you to know that they are with you and supporting you along your journey. It's now time to take the messages you've received and put them into action. Build your life and live your dreams without fear or worry. You are a beacon of light and are meant to shine and share your gifts.

When you question or feel challenged, simply reach for the book to pull a message to help give you the insight and confidence you need to push through your doubtful moment. Have faith that the Universe IS working with you and FOR you. The challenges are meant to make you stronger and the victories are there to remind you that you are on the right path.

Build your relationship with the Universe and your guides. Each time you stretch outside of your comfort zone you are growing and expanding by leaps and bounds. With each step you take you are awakening your own inner intuition even further. The messages throughout this book can serve as a constant reminder of your power and of your gift. Feel free to take some of the quotes and post them onto mirrors, inside of cabinet doors and even at on your computer monitor at home or work. They can serve as your reminder, inspiration, motivation and personal divinity coach to keep you on track!

When you feel a setback, remember to stay present. Practice mindfulness and ask the Universe what it needs for you to know at this particular crossroads in your life, then open the book to see what quote is there for you. Find the reasons to be grateful each and every day and remember to thank the Universe and your guides so that you create a new cycle of opportunity and gratitude each day.

Be well, stay well and grow well!

About the Author

Colby Rebel is an international psychic medium, #1 best-selling author of both *Psychic Senses* and *Leap Of Faith*. She is the popular podcast host of the *Colby Rebel Show* and *Coffee with Colby*. Colby is a certified master spiritual teacher through the acclaimed LWISSD where she was personally invited by world-famous psychic medium Lisa Williams. Prior to her service with Spirit, Colby worked in public accounting and taxation for fourteen years. Colby has been featured on several television programs demonstrating her gift of spirit. She is currently featured on *True Terror* with Robert Englund on the Travel Channel.

She shares her experience and knowledge for the purpose of giving you the direction, inspiration, and motivation to manifest your dreams to live your fullest life!

She currently resides in Los Angeles and is the proud owner of the *Colby Rebel Spirit Center* where she teaches and sees clients on a private basis.

Further Reading

Ask Your Guides: *Connecting to your divine support system – Sonia Choquette*

The Alchemist – Paulo Coelho

Droplets Of God: *The Life and Philosphy of Mavis Pittilla* – Suzanne Giesemann

Paul, Man of Spirit: *The World of Paul Jacobs* – Jenni Gomes

The One Thing – Gary Keller with Jay Papasan

The 50 Secrets of Self-Confidence – Richard Nugent

The 5 Second Rule – *Mel Robbins*

Power Thoughts: *365 Daily Affirmations* – Louise Hay

The Survival of the Soul and **Divine Wisdom** – Lisa Williams

Oprah's Master Class Podcast – Oprah Winfrey

Visit Colby

www.colbyrebel.com

Colby is available for keynote speaking, consultations and seminars on the topics of building a successful spiritual business and mental success. She also conducts workshops on spiritual development including intuition, psychic and mediumship.

More ways to connect with Colby:

 Email: Info@colbyrebel.com

 FB: Facebook.com/PsychicRebel

 Twitter: Twitter.com/PsychicRebel

 IG: Instagram.com/PsychicRebel

Follow Colby on FB and YouTube to watch her weekly Coffee with Colby podcast AND the Colby Rebel Show LIVE on Air!

Ready for More?

Colby offers pre-recorded trainings and online classes to help you develop your psychic and medium gifts. You can watch these in the comfort of your own home on your schedule. Build your skills and download today!

VISIT: www.ColbyRebel.com/Courses

Ready to develop your gifts? #1 Amazon Best Seller

**Psychic Senses: An Essential Guide To
Developing Your Psychic And Medium Gifts**
By: Colby Rebel

Amazon.com/Psychic-Senses-Essential-Developing-Medium/dp/057855237X/

If after reading Psychic Senses you are ready and motivated to take your gifts to the next level and have a desire to serve in a professional capacity.

Leap of Faith
How To Build Your Spiritual Business
By: Colby Rebel

Amazon.com/Leap-Faith-Build-Spiritual-Business/dp/099665318X/

Colby is a medium's medium in other words, she is one who encourages, supports and promotes other mediums in a selfless way. She is an excellent medium in her own right demonstrating throughout the world and undertaking private sessions.

She is also a modern medium utilizing social media very effectively both for herself and others, even hosting her own radio show.

I am proud to know her, to have worked with her in the past and I hope to do so in the future.

She is what all mediums should aspire to be.

—Mavis Pittilla, World Acclaimed British Medium, Former AFC Senior Tutor and Ambassador to Spirit

Thank You!

We would love to raise our cup and toast Avoca coffee roasters for their wonderful sponsorship and support!

Visit AvocaCoffee.com and order your artisan coffee beans delivered directly to your door and enjoy a fresh roasted cup while reading your daily *Coffee with Colby* Spirit Inspiration Message!

COLBY REBEL

avocacoffee.com

Printed in Great Britain
by Amazon